PRESENTS

SING LIKE AN AMERICAN IDOL!

Everything you need to sing the hits

Contents

American Idol ® 19 TV Ltd & FremantleMedia
North America, Inc.
Licensed by FremantleMedia Enterprises.
www.americanidol.com

Alfred Publishing Co., Inc.
16320 Roscoe Blvd., Suite 100
P.O. Box 10003
Van Nuys, CA 91410-0003
alfred.com

ISBN-10: 0-7390-5170-9
ISBN-13: 978-0-7390-5170-2

Introduction by DEBRA BYRD

As vocal coach and arranger for *American Idol* since Season One, I've worked with wonderful voices singing incredible songs that move them through to the next round of the competition.

This amazing collection of songs with interactive backing tracks is a tool that will enhance your talent and move you to a higher level as a vocalist. Because it allows you to prepare songs, change keys, and change the tempo, it expands your knowledge of your singing abilities. I wish something like this had been available to me when I chose to sing professionally. Even if you have no plans of singing professionally, but are looking for great songs for your own enjoyment, your singing will improve and advance by practicing with the tracks.

Finding the right song is like finding clothing that makes you look fabulous. It takes time to try on and find the perfect jeans, suit, dress, etc., and you may need alterations to get just the right fit. Take the time to find songs that are right for you. That means finding the right key, the correct tempo, and an honest story that suits you, your sound, and your talent.

The songs contained in this collection are diverse in terms of vocal ability. Some songs are quite ambitious and require a wide vocal range, while others don't. But don't be deceived. They all require an emotional connection. If there is no commitment to the heart of the song, it doesn't matter how wonderful you sound.

First impressions are lasting. It takes practice, courage, strength, and ambition, at any age, to make a great presentation. When you audition, the people "on the other side of the table" want to be thrilled, and your audience wants you to be wonderful.

There are basic tools you need for each song and every phrase to sing your best. Great **posture** means standing tall to align your body, with shoulders back, chest high, and one foot slightly in front of the other. It may feel awkward, but, in time, you will master it.

Practice lining up your body on a wall. Make sure your spine is straight as you stand tall and touches the wall at three points of your body: your head, back, and buttocks should make contact on the wall.

It's important to remember that if you decide to sit while singing, whether on a chair at rehearsal, on a high stool, or on the edge of a stage, the same posture principles apply. Sit up. Correct alignment puts all the muscles you need to sing in the right position to help you sing better, plus you look more confident and professional. Practice maintaining your posture when you walk. You don't have to be as stiff as a board, but soon it will become second nature, and you'll be in correct alignment when you move.

Because you've learned to align your body properly, it makes you aware of being relaxed while singing. **Tension** can cause strain and discomfort. Be aware of tightening your body when practicing. Release tension in your neck, chest, back, jaw, forehead, and arms. You'll breathe easier, and your sound will be more open.

Breathing correctly is essential, because you have to take in enough air to get you through a long phrase. It's also important for projection, volume, and controlling your tone or sound. Inhale as if you're blowing up a balloon. As you take in air slowly to the count of four, you can feel your abdomen and back expand. Your stomach will pooch out, and you'll feel your rib cage part. Your chest should remain still, and make sure your shoulders stay relaxed and don't move up toward your ears, because that creates tension in your neck and back. As you exhale slowly, you'll feel your abdomen go into its normal place, and your rib cage and back will relax to their normal positions. Do a few repetitions without singing, then sing and monitor your breathing.

You may be yawning more than you normally do. That's because you're learning a deeper breathing technique, and you have an open throat which will trigger a yawn reflex. It's a good thing.

Practice every day. It takes time and determination to learn the ABC's of breath control. Be patient. When breathing correctly while you sing becomes a habit, pay attention to how you breathe when speaking. With

DEBRA BYRD is the vocal coach and arranger for every season of American Idol and for seasons 2 thru 6 of Canadian Idol. She coached the 2006-2007 tour of High School Musical-The Concert and the My Grammy Moment Contest with Justin Timberlake for the 49th Annual Grammy Awards and 2007 MTV Movie Awards. Byrd has recorded duets with Barry Manilow and Bob Dylan, has been featured in five Broadway shows and movie soundtracks. She is vocal arranger for Manilow's Emmy award winning Music and Passion in Las Vegas. Her DVD, Vocal Help Now! and seminars "Welcome To STAR SCHOOL" offer important advice on how to improve and protect your voice and ace auditions.

Photo by Lisa Stahl Sullivan

www.debrabyrd.com

practice and awareness, these breathing fundamentals become second nature, and you won't have to think about it all the time.

Tone quality is important because your sound is unique to you. Some singers try to imitate their favorites. It's important that you sound like *you*. The songs in this great collection were originally recorded and sung by some of the most outstanding vocalists of our time. With practice, you can develop a voice that is just as impressive. But you must practice!

Your unique sound should be a natural extension of your speaking voice, so it's very important you sing within your **vocal range**. If a song is very "rangy," meaning it has low notes as well as high notes, it's not a good song choice for you if you don't sing those notes comfortably. For example, sopranos don't always have the ability to sing very low notes. Kelly Clarkson, an incredible singer, has expanded her range since being a contestant on

American Idol. At that time, her lowest note was middle C.

At dress rehearsal early in Season One, *Idol* judge Randy Jackson was concerned because Kelly altered notes for the beginning of a song she had chosen. I explained to him that the beginning of the song was completely out of her range, and I remember his surprise when I explained that Kelly's lowest note was middle C. Because she knew her limits and didn't force her singing, her amazing musicality shone through.

George Huff, a marvelous singer from Season Three, came into the competition abruptly after another contestant left, and he made it to the Top 10; however, he came in with only about 55 percent of his vocal ability because he had been ill. He fought to maintain his unique tonal quality by being extremely disciplined and not pushing his voice or his range during the entire contest. Every week, he would say, "It's coming back,

Byrd, it's coming back!" And his voice did come back. I applaud George for knowing his limits and being a smart singer.

Regarding **auditions**, the most important thing to do before an audition is be prepared. Always wake up your body and warm up your voice before the audition. You need energy and focus to do well. Eat a good meal; overeating will make you feel sluggish, but you need fuel for energy. Your body is your instrument, and you get out of it what you put into it. It's not smart to jump out of bed and go sing.

Deciding **what to sing** is huge and shouldn't be taken for granted. Your song choice should be appropriate for the type of audition. Do they want rock, musical theater, a standard, something classical, the blues, an aria, gospel, etc.? For *American Idol*, it's up to you to show who you are as an artist with the songs you've chosen. What type of singer are you? What style of music would you record to be the next new thing? Is it rock, country, R & B, pop?

Chris Daughtry was very confident about his style of singing before he auditioned for *American Idol*. During the competition, he fine tuned his conviction of who he is as an artist. The same could be said about Carrie Underwood. At rehearsal, she told me she wanted to be known for singing country rock songs. Her hit record, *Before He Cheats*, totally embraces her vision of herself as a successful artist.

Even if you choose songs you've known for years, it takes **practice** to refresh your memory of the lyrics, melody, and the sections you'd like to sing, because you may not be asked to sing the entire song. But, make sure you know the entire song; they just might ask you to do it. Polish an up-tempo and a ballad, plus have a third song ready, just in case. Be prepared to sing a verse and a chorus. In musical theater, you may be asked to "give me sixteen bars" or "I'd like to hear the money notes!"

One thing is certain, they all want **emotion**. Learn your lyrics line by line, section by section. Knowing the story will help you understand the song. As you sing, tune into the feeling it's expressing, and build it into your performance. After you've learned all that, go back and do it again, this time in front of a mirror. Next, sing it for a family member or a friend who will tell you the truth. This lets you realize how others see you. Being fully prepared is essential, because there's a lot to think about while you're performing, and plenty of distractions. Focus on your song and how you present it. As you relax into the song, your tension and jitters begin to disappear.

Whether singing to the tracks included with the songbook, with a pianist, or a cappella, it's important to **be prepared**. No excuses. Keep your eyes open; you're the storyteller. Don't be nervous; be focused, and enjoy the ride!

AGAINST ALL ODDS
(Take a Look at Me Now)

Words and Music by
PHIL COLLINS

Against All Odds - 4 - 1

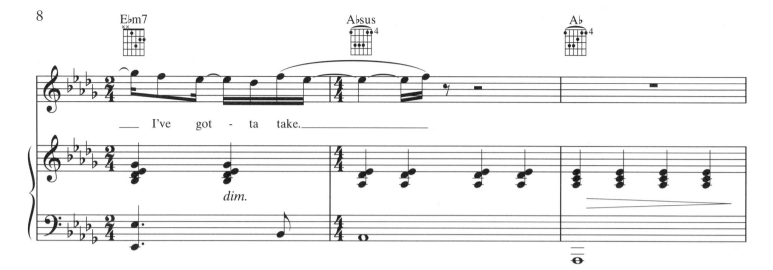

I've got - ta take.

Take a look at me now.

Verse 2:
How can you just walk away from me,
When all I can do is watch you leave?
'Cause you shared the laughter and the pain,
And even shared the tears.
You're the only one who really knew me at all.
(To Chorus 1:)

Verse 3:
I wish I could just make you turn around,
Turn around and see me cry.
There's so much I need to say to you,
So many reasons why.
You're the only one who really knew me at all.
(To Chorus 2:)

ALWAYS ON MY MIND

Words and Music by
WAYNE THOMPSON, MARK JAMES
and JOHNNY CHRISTOPHER

Gtr. tuned down 1/2 step:
⑥ = E♭ ③ = G♭
⑤ = A♭ ② = B♭
④ = D♭ ① = E♭

AMAZED

Words and Music by
MARV GREEN, AIMEE MAYO
and CHRIS LINDSEY

(with pedal)

1. Ev-'ry time our eyes meet, this feel-ing in-side me is al-most more__ than I can
2. *See additional lyrics*

take. Ba-by, when you touch me, I can feel how much you love me,

Amazed - 5 - 1

14

Verse 2:
The smell of your skin,
The taste of your kiss,
The way you whisper in the dark.
Your hair all around me,
Baby, you surround me;
You touch every place in my heart.
Though it feels like the first time every time,
I wanna spend the whole night in your eyes.
(To Chorus:)

BLESS THE BROKEN ROAD

Words and Music by
JEFF HANNA, MARCUS HUMMON
and BOBBY BOYD

Bless the Broken Road - 7 - 1

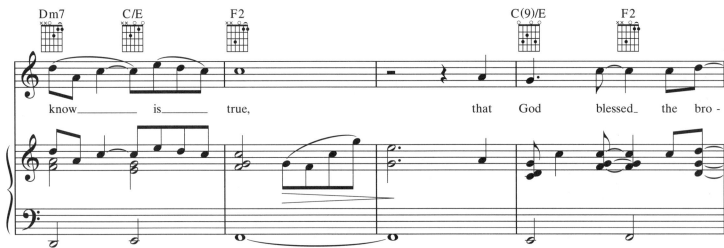

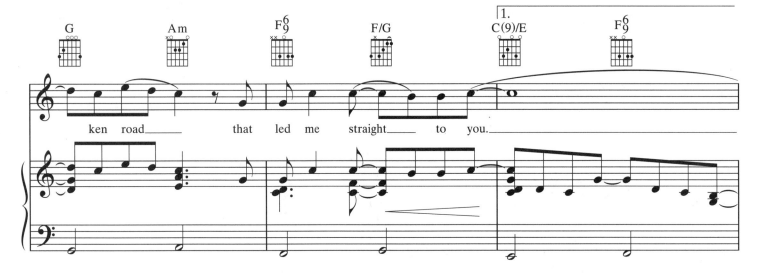

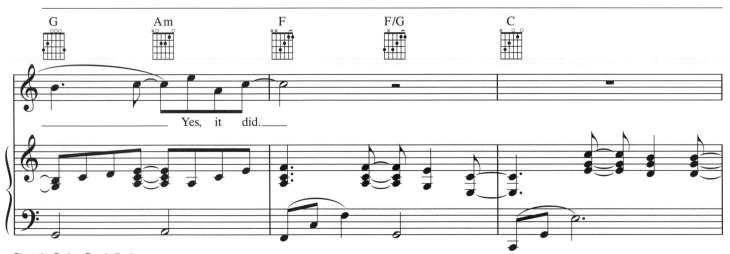

22

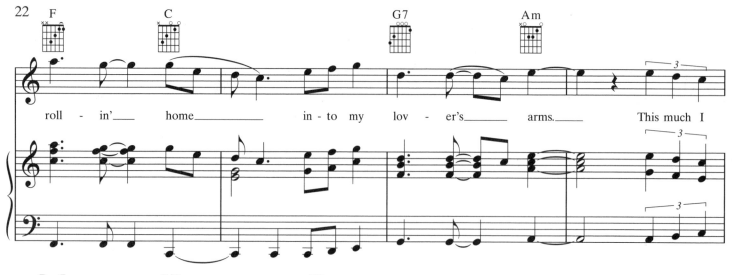

roll - in'____ home_____ in - to my lov - er's_____ arms._____ This much I

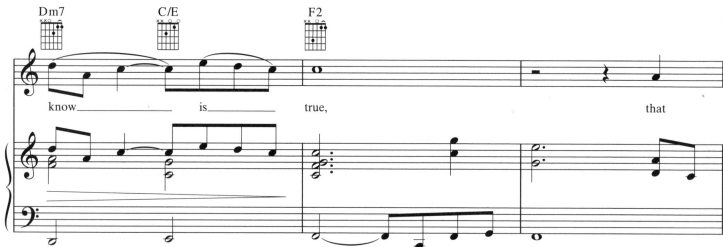

know_____ is_____ true, that

God blessed__ the bro - ken road_____ that led me straight_____ to you,__

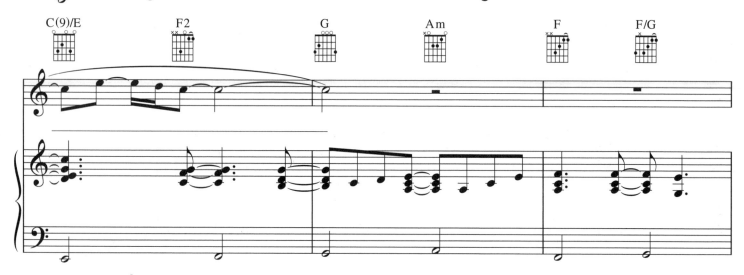

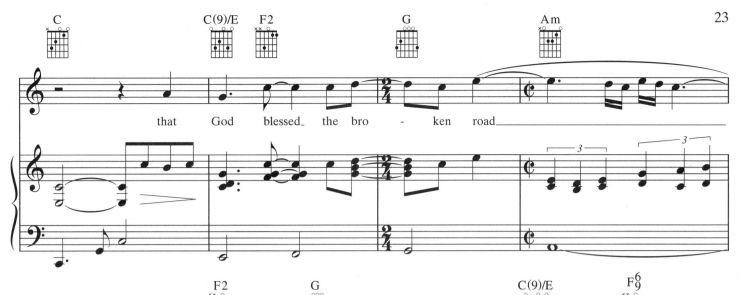

that God blessed_ the bro - ken road_____

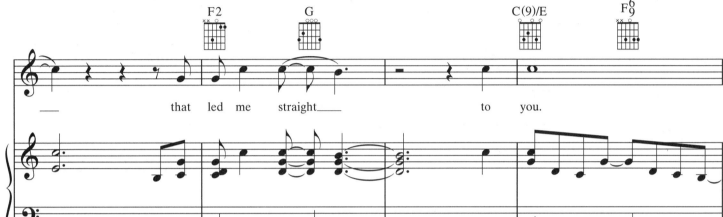

__ that led me straight____ to you.

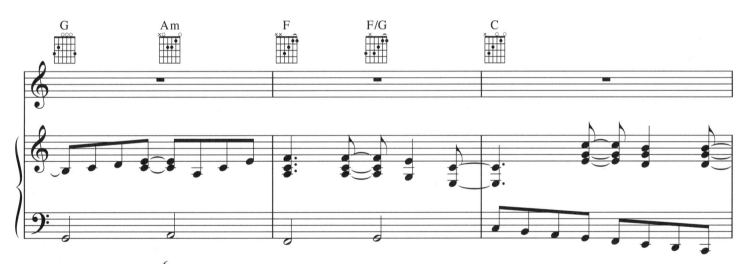

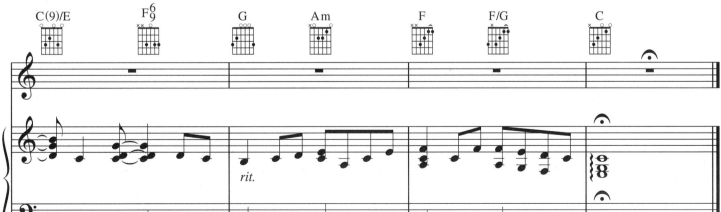

rit.

DESPERADO

Words and Music by
DON HENLEY and GLENN FREY

Desperado - 6 - 1

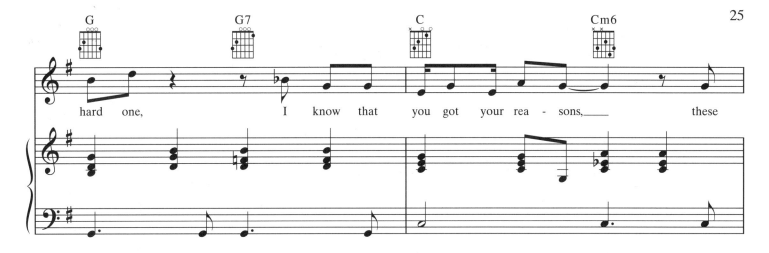

hard one, I know that you got your rea - sons,____ these

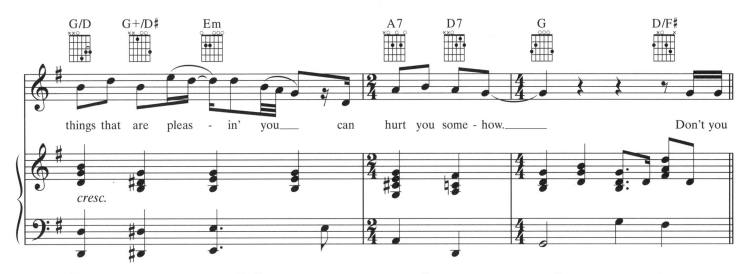

things that are pleas - in' you____ can hurt you some - how._____ Don't you

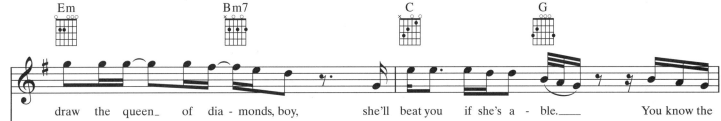

draw the queen_ of dia - monds, boy, she'll beat you if she's a - ble.____ You know the

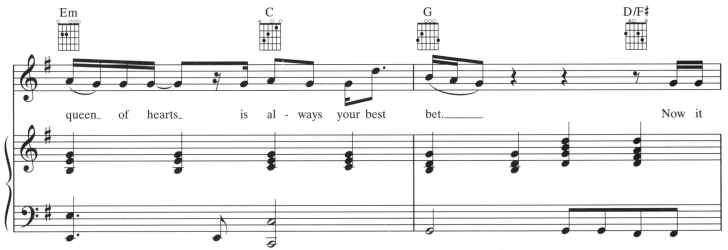

queen_ of hearts_ is al - ways your best bet._____ Now it

Desperado - 6 - 2

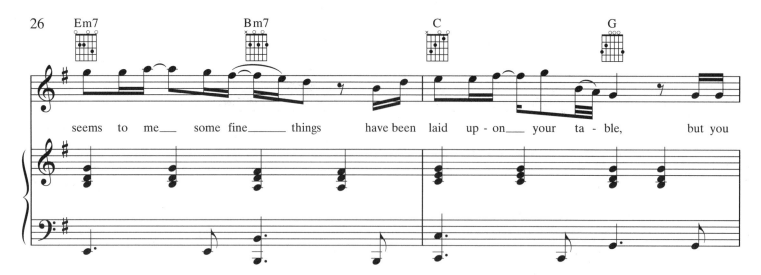

seems to me___ some fine_____ things have been laid up-on___ your ta-ble, but you

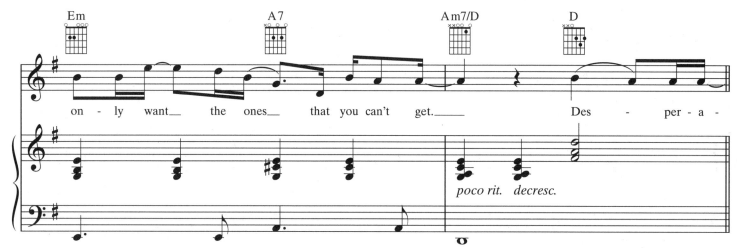

on - ly want___ the ones___ that you can't get._____ Des - per - a -

poco rit. decresc.

do, oh, you ain't get-tin' no young - er, your

a tempo

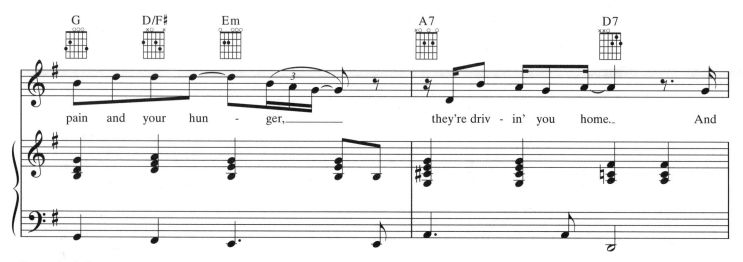

pain and your hun - ger,_____ they're driv - in' you home.__ And

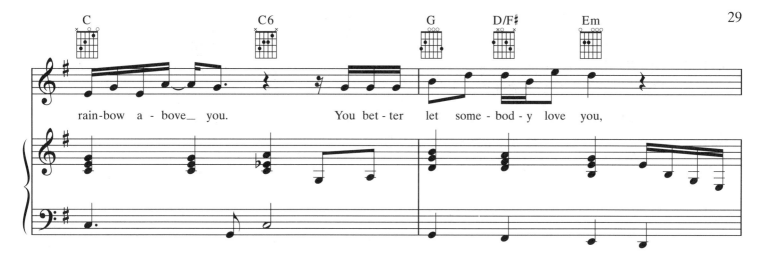

rain-bow a - bove_ you. You bet - ter let some - bod - y love you,

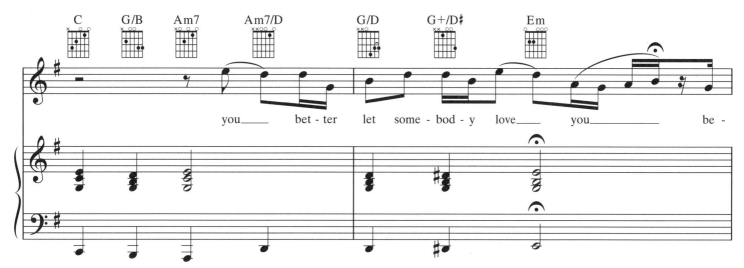

you___ bet - ter let some - bod - y love___ you___ be -

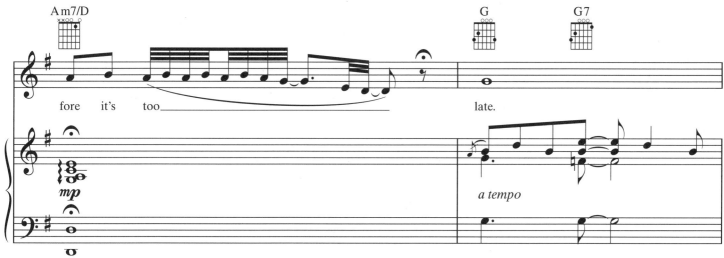

fore it's too___ late.

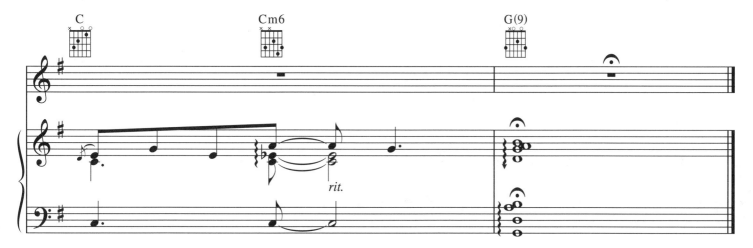

Desperado - 6 - 6

(EVERYTHING I DO) I DO IT FOR YOU

Words and Music by
BRYAN ADAMS, ROBERT JOHN "MUTT" LANGE
and MICHAEL KAMEN

(Everything I Do) I Do for You - 4 - 1

HOME

Words and Music by
MICHAEL BUBLÉ, AMY FOSTER-GILLIES
and ALAN CHANG

Home - 6 - 1

Home - 6 - 4

HOW YOU REMIND ME

Drop D tuning: ⑥ = D

Lyrics by CHAD KROEGER
Music by NICKELBACK

Moderately slow ♩ = 86

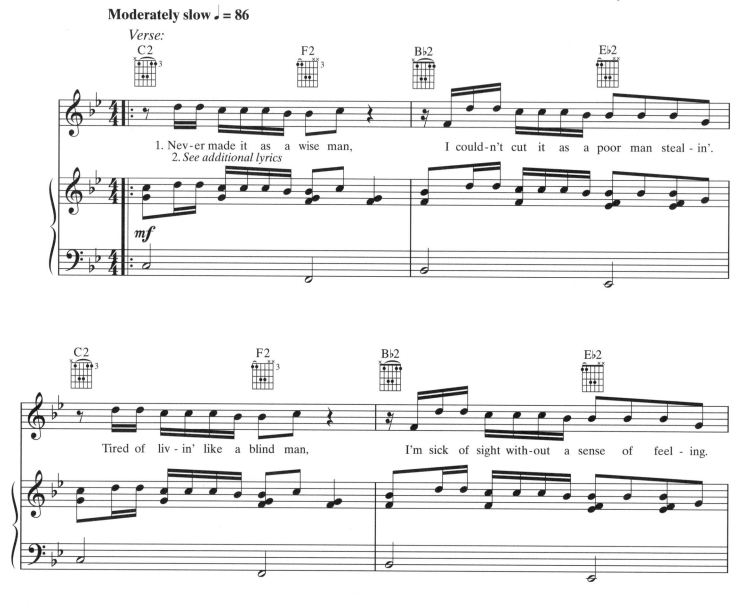

Verse:

1. Nev-er made it as a wise man, I could-n't cut it as a poor man steal-in'.
2. See additional lyrics

Tired of liv-in' like a blind man, I'm sick of sight with-out a sense of feel-ing.

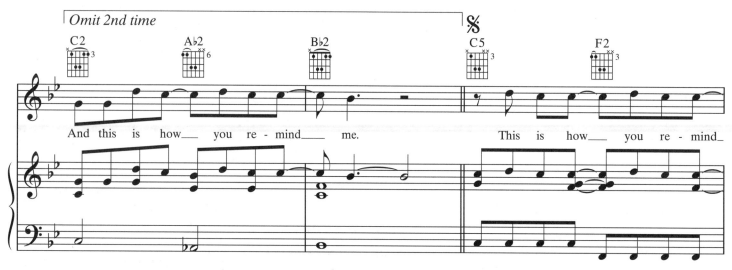

Omit 2nd time

And this is how___ you re-mind___ me. This is how___ you re-mind___

How You Remind Me - 5 - 1

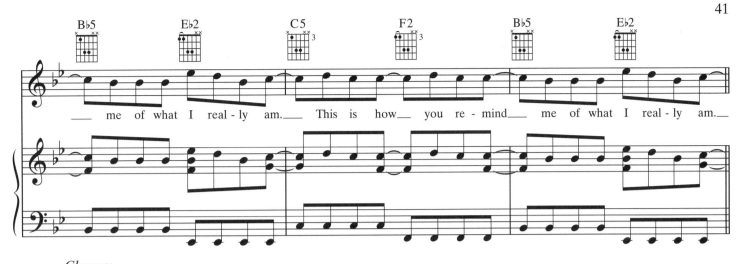

Chorus:

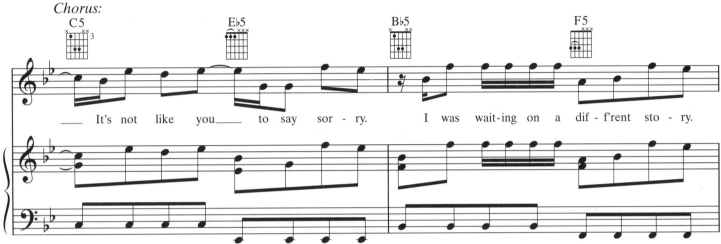

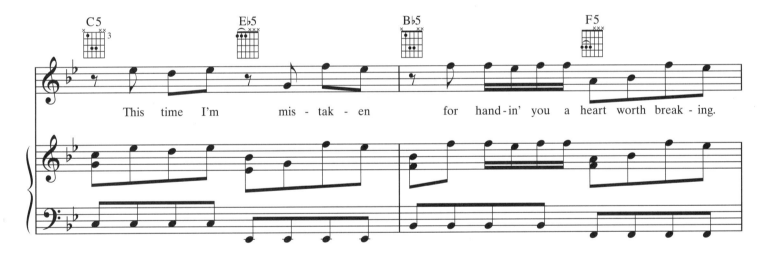

To Coda ⊕

These five words___ in my head scream, "Are we hav-in' fun___ yet?"___

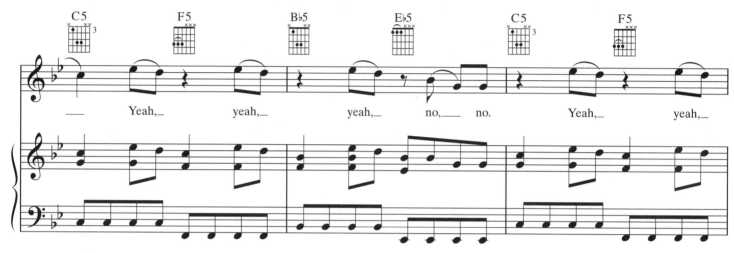

___ Yeah,___ yeah,___ yeah,___ no,___ no. Yeah,___ yeah,___

1.   2.

yeah,___ no,___ no.   yeah,___ no,___ no. Yeah,___ yeah,___

yeah,___ no,___ no. Yeah,___ yeah,___ yeah,___ no,___ no.

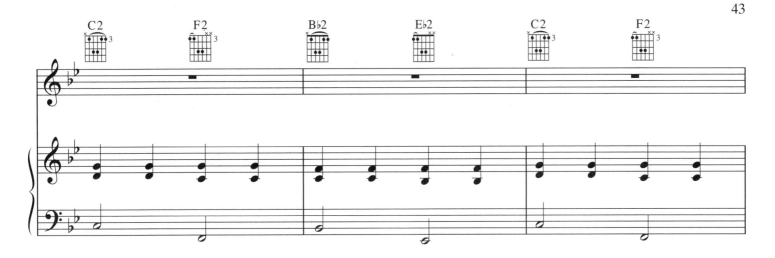

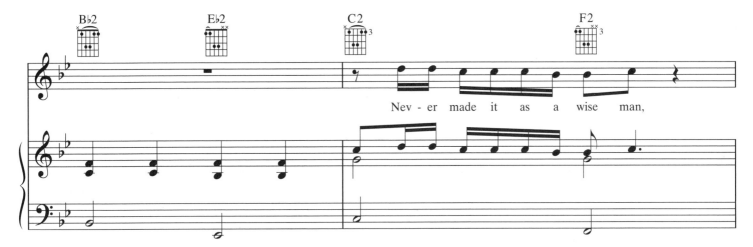

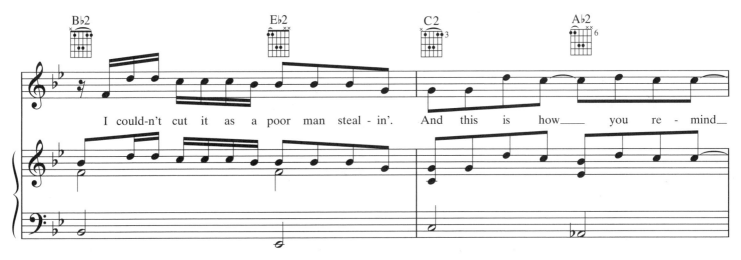

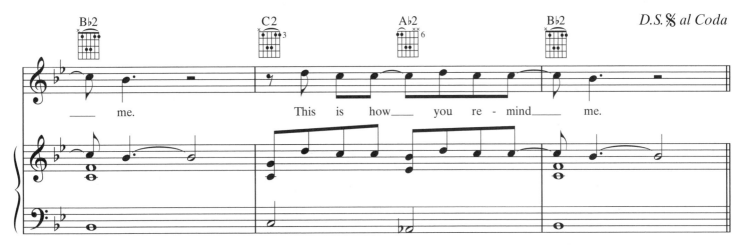

44

Yeah,— yeah,— are we hav-in' fun— yet?

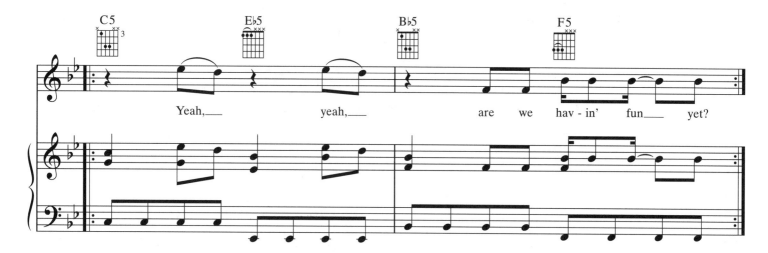

Yeah,— yeah,— are we hav-in' fun— yet?

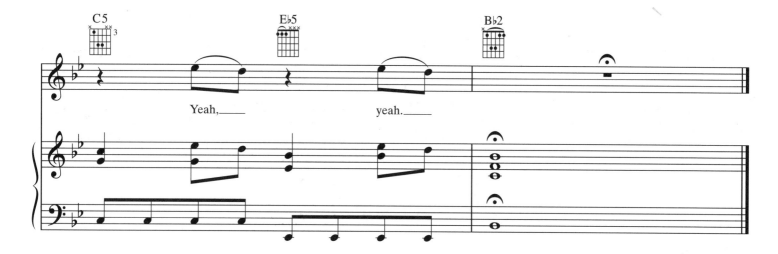

Yeah,— yeah.—

Verse 2:
It's not like you didn't know that.
I said I love you and swear I still do.
And it must have been so bad,
'Cause livin' with me must have damn near killed you.
This is how you remind me of what I really am.
This is how you remind me of what I really am.
(To Chorus:)

I DON'T WANT TO BE

Words and Music by
GAVIN DeGRAW

Moderately slow ♩ = 76

I Don't Want to Be - 5 - 1

Bridge:

Can I have ev - 'ry-one's at - ten-tion, please?—

(Spoken:) If you're not like this and that, you're gonna have to leave.

I came from the moun - tain, the crust of cre - a - tion.

D.S. %S al Coda

My whole sit - u - a - tion made from clay to stone, and now I'm tell - in' ev - 'ry - bod - y.

MACK THE KNIFE

English Words by
MARC BLITZSTEIN
Original German Words by
BERT BRECHT

Music by
KURT WEILL

Mack the Knife - 7 - 1

52

54

56

OPEN ARMS

Words and Music by
STEVE PERRY and
JONATHAN CAIN

Chorus:

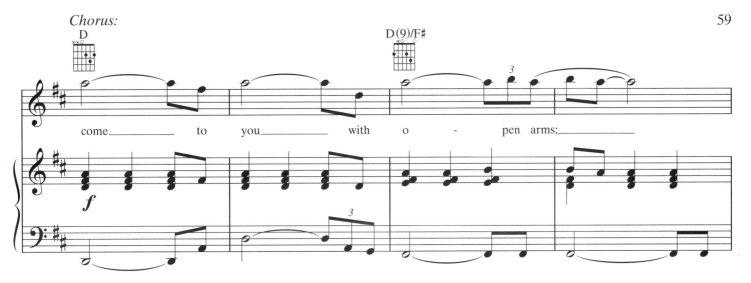

come_____ to you_____ with o - pen arms;_____

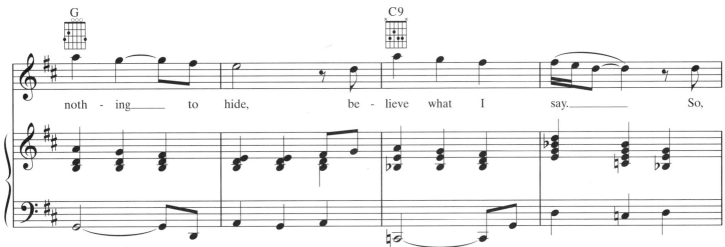

noth - ing_____ to hide, be - lieve what I say._____ So,

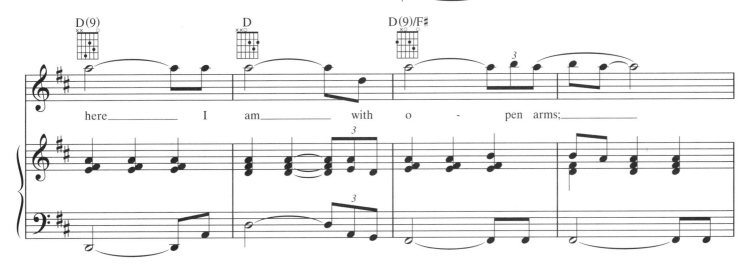

here_____ I am_____ with o - pen arms;_____

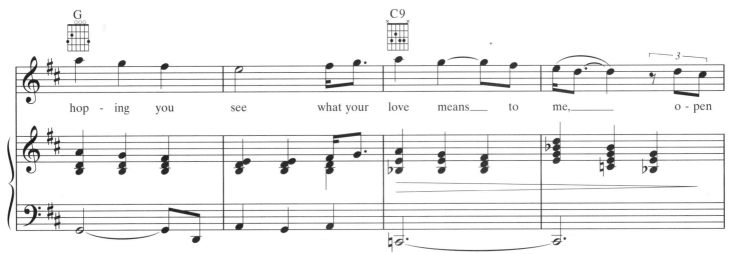

hop - ing you see what your love means___ to me,_____ o - pen

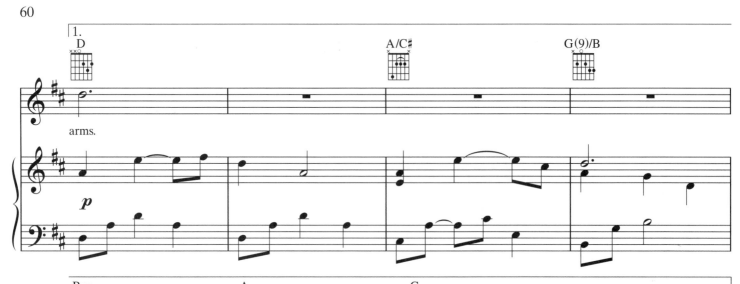

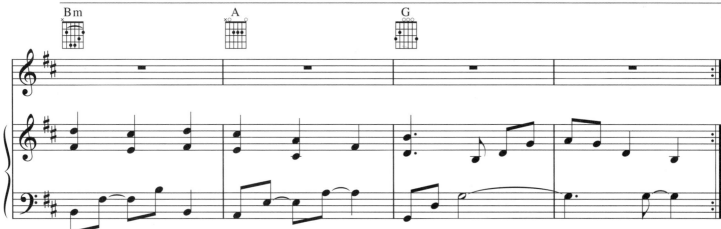

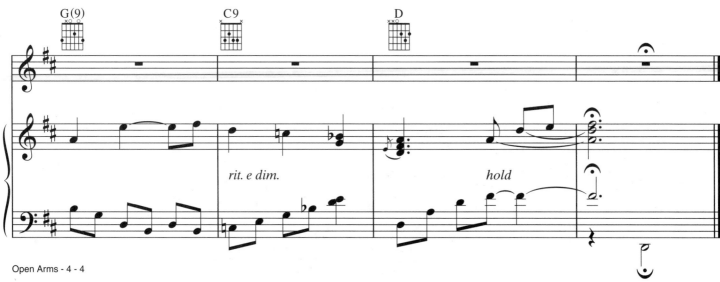

WHAT A WONDERFUL WORLD

Words and Music by
GEORGE DAVID WEISS and BOB THIELE

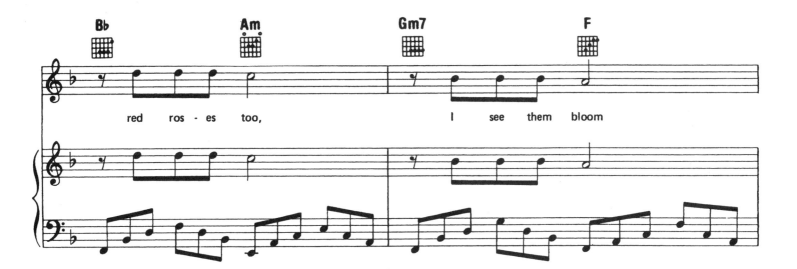

What a Wonderful World - 4 - 1

64

What a Wonderful World - 4 - 4

SMOOTH

Music and Lyrics by
ITAAL SHUR and ROB THOMAS

Smooth - 5 - 1

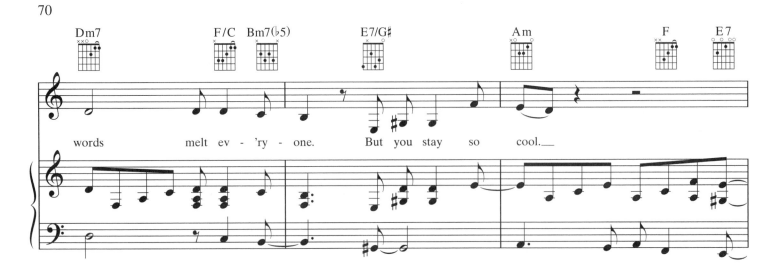

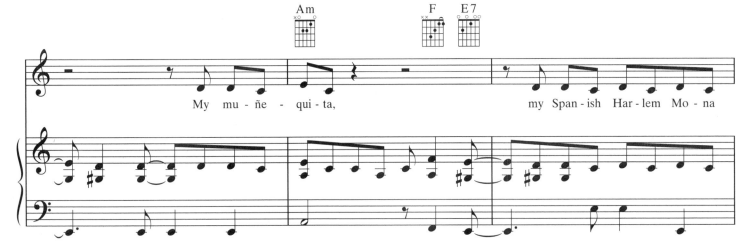

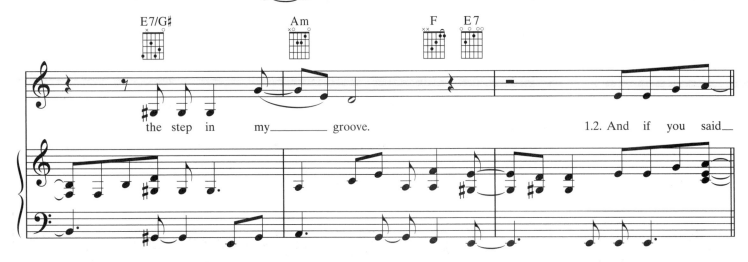

same as the e-mo-tion that I get from you.____ You got the kind of lov-ing that can

To Coda ⊕ |1.

be so smooth,_ yeah. Give me your heart,_ make it real,____ or else for-get a-bout it.

|2.
N.C.

D.S. ℅ *al Coda*

2. Well, I'll tell you ____ or else for-get a-bout it.

Smooth - 5 - 4

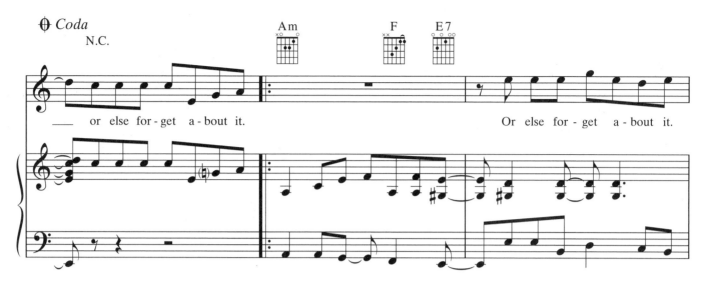

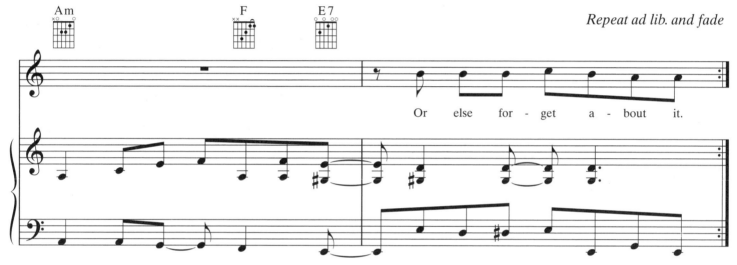

Verse 2:
Well, I'll tell you one thing,
If you would leave, it be a crying shame.
In every breath and every word
I hear your name calling me out, yeah.
Well, out from the barrio,
You hear my rhythm on your radio.
You feel the tugging of the world,
So soft and slow, turning you 'round and 'round.
(To Pre-chorus:)

WHEN A MAN LOVES A WOMAN

Words and Music by
CALVIN LEWIS and ANDREW WRIGHT

When a Man Loves a Woman - 5 - 1

When a Man Loves a Woman - 5 - 2

76

Ba - by, ba - by, please___ don't treat me bad.___   3. When a

Verse 3:

man___ loves a wom - an,   deep down in his soul,___

she can bring him___ such mis - e - ry.___   If she is

playing him___ for a fool,___   he's the last one to know.

WHEN THE STARS GO BLUE

Words and Music by
RYAN ADAMS

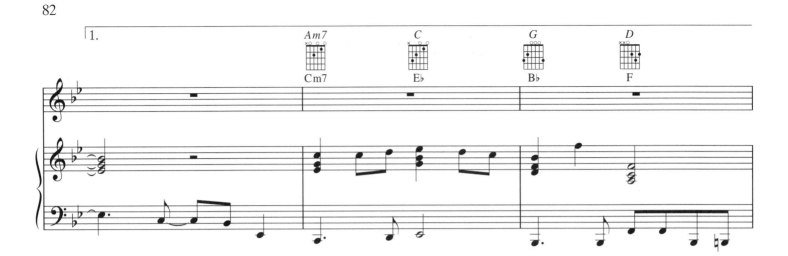

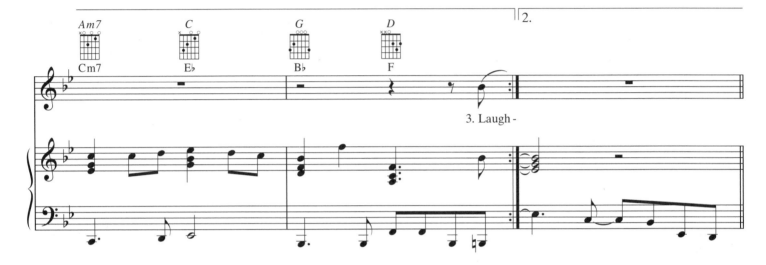

3. Laugh -

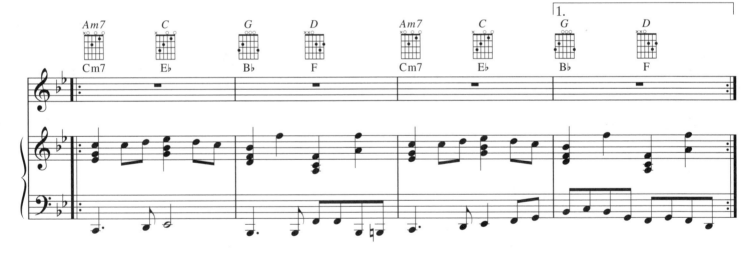

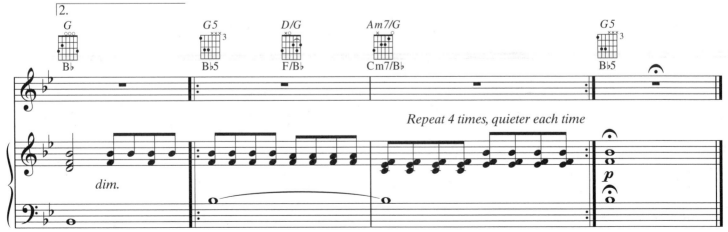

Repeat 4 times, quieter each time

dim.

p

YOU RAISE ME UP

Words and Music by
ROLF LOVLAND and
BRENDAN GRAHAM

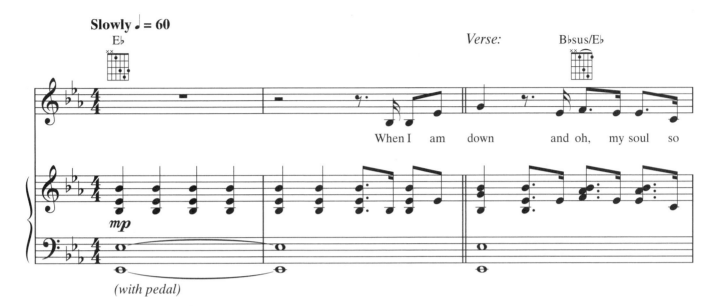

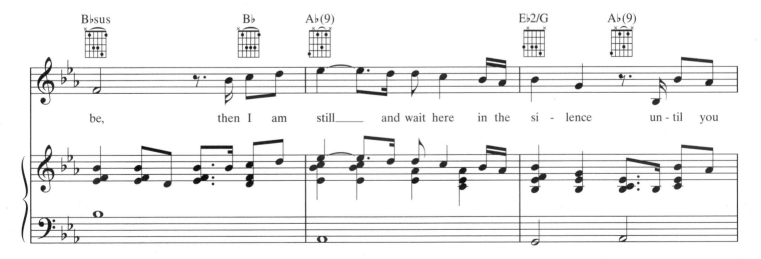

You Raise Me Up - 5 - 1

Chorus:

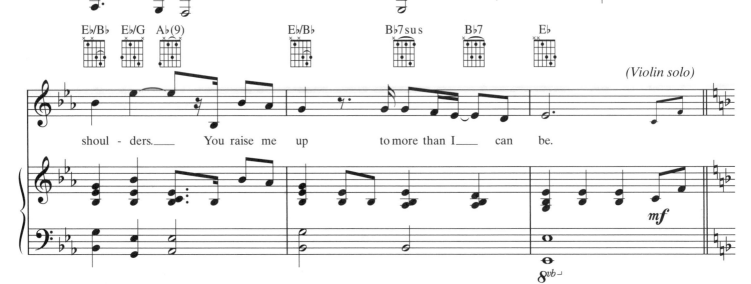

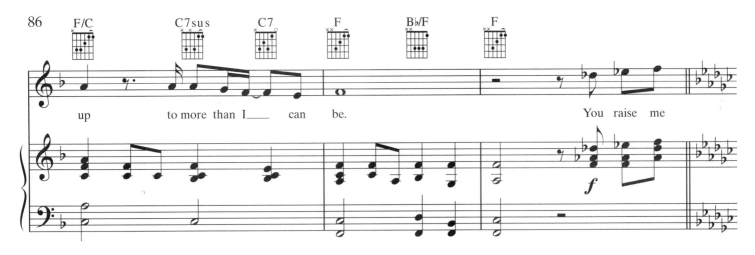

Chorus:

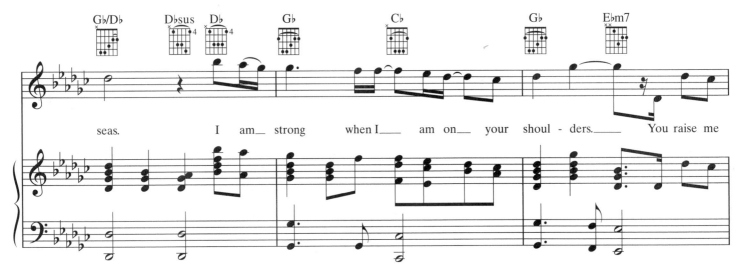

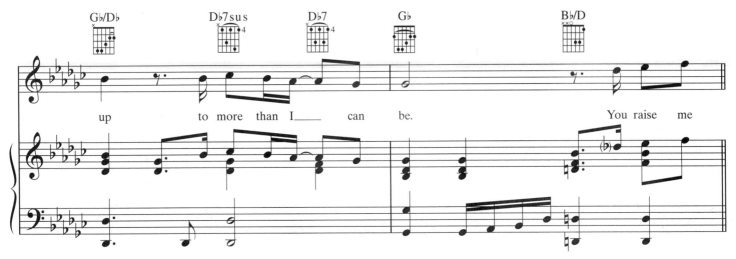

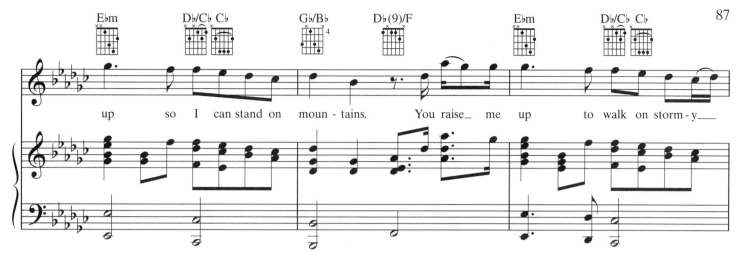

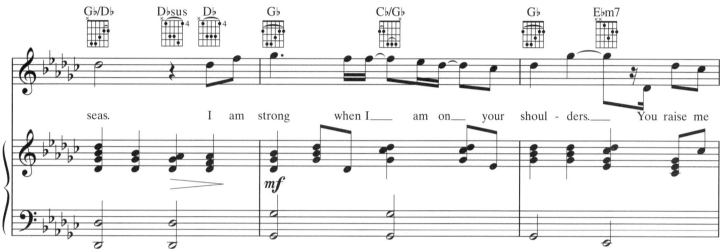

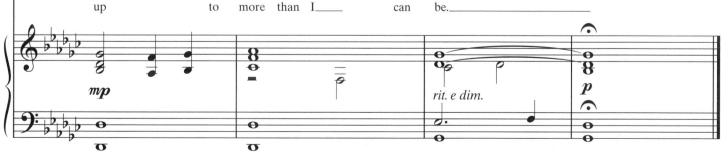

AGAINST ALL ODDS (TAKE A LOOK AT ME NOW)

(From the movie "Against All Odds")
Words and Music by PHIL COLLINS

Verse 1:
How can I just let you walk away,
Just let you leave without a trace?
When I stand here taking every breath
With you; ooh,
You're the only one
Who really knew me at all.

Verse 2:
How can you just walk away from me,
When all I can do is watch you leave?
'Cause you shared the laughter and the pain,
And even shared the tears.
You're the only one
Who really knew me at all.

Chorus 1:
So take a look at me now,
Well, there's just an empty space.
And there's nothing left here to remind me,
Just the memory of your face.
Well, take a look at me now,
Well, there's just an empty space.
And you comin' back to me
Is against the odds,
And that's what I've got to face.

Verse 3:
I wish I could just make you turn around,
Turn around and see me cry.
There's so much I need to say to you,
So many reasons why.
You're the only one
Who really knew me at all.

Chorus 2:
So take a look at me now,
Well, there's just an empty space.
And there's nothing left here to remind me,
Just the memory of your face.
Now, take a look at me now,
'Cause there's just an empty space.
But to wait for you is all I can do,
And that's what I've gotta face.

Chorus 3:
Take a good look at me now,
'Cause I'll still be standing here.
And you coming back to me
Is against all odds,
It's the chance I've gotta take.
Take a look at me now.

ALWAYS ON MY MIND

(In the style of Willie Nelson)
Words and Music by WAYNE THOMPSON, MARK JAMES and JOHNNY CHRISTOPHER

Verse 1:
Maybe I didn't love you
Quite as often as I could have.
And maybe I didn't treat you
Quite as good as I should have.
If I made you feel second best,
Girl, I'm sorry, I was blind.
You were always on my mind,
You were always on my mind.

Verse 2:
And maybe I didn't hold you
All those lonely, lonely times.
And I guess I never told you
I'm so happy that you're mine.
Little things I should have said and done,
I just never took the time.
You were always on my mind,
You were always on my mind.

Bridge:
Tell me, tell me that
Your sweet love hasn't died.
And give me,
Give me one more chance
To keep you satisfied,
I'll keep you satisfied.

Verse 3:
(Instrumental solo 8 bars)
Little things I should have said and done,
I just never took the time.
You were always on my mind,
You were always on my mind.
You were always on my mind,
You were always on my mind.

AMAZED

(In the style of Lonestar)
Words and Music by MARV GREEN, AIMEE MAYO and CHRIS LINDSEY

Verse 1:
Every time our eyes meet,
This feeling inside me
Is almost more than I can take.
Baby, when you touch me,
I can feel how much you love me,
And it just blows me away.
I've never been this close
To anyone or anything.
I can hear your thoughts,
I can see your dreams.

Chorus:
I don't know how you do what you do.
I'm so in love with you.
It just keeps getting better.
I wanna spend the rest of my life
With you by my side
Forever and ever.
And every little thing that you do,
Baby, I'm amazed by you.

Verse 2:
The smell of your skin,
The taste of your kiss,
The way you whisper in the dark.
Your hair all around me,
Baby, you surround me;
You touch every place in my heart.
Though it feels like the first time every time,
I wanna spend the whole night in your eyes.

Chorus:
I don't know how you do what you do.
I'm so in love with you.
It just keeps getting better.
I wanna spend the rest of my life
With you by my side
Forever and ever.
Every little thing that you do,
Baby, I'm amazed by you.

Chorus:
Every little thing that you do,
I'm so in love with you.
It just keeps getting better.
I wanna spend the rest of my life
With you by my side
Forever and ever.
Every little thing that you do, oh,
Every little thing that you do,
Baby, I'm amazed by you.

BLESS THE BROKEN ROAD

(In the style of Rascal Flatts)
Words and Music by JEFF HANNA, MARCUS HUMMON and BOBBY BOYD

Verse 1:
I set out on a narrow way
Many years ago,
Hoping I would find true love
Along the broken road.
But I got lost a time or two,
Wiped my brow and kept pushin' through.
I couldn't see how every sign
Pointed straight to you.

Chorus:
Every long-lost dream
Led me to where you are.
Others who broke my heart,
They were like northern stars,
Pointin' me on my way
Into your loving arms.
This much I know is true,
That God blessed the broken road
That led me straight to you.
Yes, it did.

Verse 2:
I think about the years I've spent
Just passin' through.
I'd like to have the time I lost
And give it back to you.
But you just smile and take my hand.
You've been there, you understand.
It's all part of a grander plan
That is comin' true.

Chorus:
Every long-lost dream
Led me to where you are.
Others who broke my heart,
They were like northern stars,
Pointin' me on my way
Into your loving arms.
This much I know is true,
That God blessed the broken road
That led me straight to you.
Yeah, hey, yeah.

Now I'm just a-rollin' home
Into my lover's arms.
This much I know is true,
That God blessed the broken road
That led me straight to you,
That God blessed the broken road
That led me straight to you.

DESPERADO

(As recorded by Eagles)
Words and Music by DON HENLEY and GLENN FREY

Desperado, why don't you come to your senses?
You been out ridin' fences for so long now.
Oh, you're a hard one,
I know that you got your reasons,
These things that are pleasin' you
Can hurt you somehow.

Don't you draw the queen of diamonds, boy,
She'll beat you if she's able.
You know the queen of hearts is always your best bet.
Now it seems to me some fine things
Have been laid upon upon your table,
But you only want the ones that you can't get.

Desperado, oh, you ain't gettin' no younger,
Your pain and your hunger, they're drivin' you home.
And freedom, oh, freedom,
Well, that's just some people talkin'.
Your prison is walkin' through this world all alone.

Don't your feet get cold in the wintertime?
The sky won't snow and the sun won't shine.
It's hard to tell the nighttime from the day.
You're losin' all your highs and lows.
Ain't it funny how the feeling goes away?

Desperado, why don't you come to your senses?
Come down from your fences, open the gate.
It may be rainin', but there's a rainbow above you.
You better let somebody love you,
You better let somebody love you before it's too late.

(EVERYTHING I DO) I DO IT FOR YOU

(As recorded by Bryan Adams)
Lyrics and Music by BRYAN ADAMS, ROBERT JOHN LANGE and MICHAEL KAMEN

Look into my eyes, you will see
What you mean to me.
Search your heart, search your soul,
And when you find me there you'll search no more.
Don't tell me it's not worth fighting for.
You can't tell me it's not worth dying for.
You know it's true, ev'rything I do, I do it for you.

Look into your heart, you will find
There's nothing there to hide.
So take me as I am, take my life,
I would give it all, I would sacrifice.
Don't tell me it's not worth fighting for.
I can't help it, there's nothing I want more.
You know it's true, ev'rything I do, I do it for you.

There's no love like your love,
And no other could give more love.
There's no way, unless you're there all the time,
All the way, yeah.

Oh, you can't tell me it's not worth trying for.
I can't help it, there's nothing I want more.
Yeah, I would fight for you, I'd lie for you,
Walk the mile for you, yeah, I'd die for you.
You know it's true, ev'rything I do,
Oh, oh, I do it for you.

HOME

(In the style of Michael Bublé)
Words and Music by MICHAEL BUBLÉ, AMY FOSTER-GILLIES and ALAN CHANG

Verse:
Another summer day has come and gone away
In Paris and Rome, but I wanna go home.
May be surrounded by a million people,
I still feel all alone, just wanna go home.
Oh, I miss you, you know.

I've been keeping all the letters that I wrote to you,
Each one a line or two,
"I'm fine, baby. How are you?"
Well, I would send them,
But I know that it's just not enough.
My words were cold and flat,
And you deserve more than that.

Another aeroplane, another sunny place.
I'm lucky, I know, but I wanna go home.
I've got to go home.

Chorus:
Let me go home.
I'm just too far from where you are,
I wanna come home.

Verse:
And I feel just like I'm living someone else's life.
It's like I just stepped outside,
When ev'rything was going right.
And I know just why you couldn't come along with me.
This was not your dream,
But you always believed in me.

Another winter day has come and gone away
In either Paris or Rome, and I wanna go home.
Let me go home.

Coda:
And I'm surrounded by a million people, I,
I still feel alone, oh, let me go home.
Oh, I miss you, you know.

Chorus:
Let me go home.
I've had my run, and, baby, I'm done.
I've gotta go home. Let me go home.
It'll be alright, I'll be home tonight.
I'm coming back home.

HOW YOU REMIND ME

(In the style of Nickelback)
Lyrics by CHAD KROEGER
Music by NICKELBACK

Verse 1:
Never made it as a wise man,
I couldn't cut it as a poor man stealin'.
Tired of livin' like a blind man,
I'm sick of sight without a sense of feeling.
And this is how you remind me.
This is how
You remind me of what I really am.
This is how
You remind me of what I really am.

Chorus:
It's not like you to say sorry.
I was waiting on a diff'rent story.
This time I'm mistaken
For handin' you a heart worth breaking.
And I've been wrong, I've been down,
Been to the bottom of every bottle.
These five words in my head scream,
"Are we havin' fun yet?"

Yeah, yeah, yeah, no, no.
Yeah, yeah, yeah, no, no.

Verse 2:
It's not like you didn't know that.
I said I love you and I swear I still do.
And it must have been so bad,
'Cause livin' with me
Must have damn near killed you.
This is how
You remind me of what I really am.
This is how
You remind me of what I really am.

Chorus:
It's not like you to say sorry.
I was waiting on a diff'rent story.
This time I'm mistaken
For handin' you a heart worth breaking.
And I've been wrong, I've been down,
Been to the bottom of every bottle.
These five words in my head scream,
"Are we havin' fun yet?"

Yeah, yeah, yeah, no, no.
Yeah, yeah, yeah, no, no.
Yeah, yeah, yeah, no, no.
Yeah, yeah, yeah, no, no.

Never made it as a wise man,
I couldn't cut it as a poor man stealin'.
And this is how you remind me.
This is how you remind me.

Chorus:
It's not like you to say sorry.
I was waiting on a diff'rent story.
This time I'm mistaken
For handin' you a heart worth breaking.
And I've been wrong, I've been down,
Been to the bottom of every bottle.
These five words in my head scream,
"Are we havin' fun yet?"

Yeah, yeah, are we havin' fun yet?
Yeah, yeah, are we havin' fun yet?
Yeah, yeah, are we havin' fun yet?
Yeah, yeah.

I DON'T WANT TO BE

(In the style of Gavin DeGraw)
Words and Music by GAVIN DeGRAW

Verse 1:
I don't need to be anything other
Than a prison guard's son.
I don't need to be anything other
Than a specialist's son.
I don't have to be anyone other
Than the birth of two souls in one.
Part of where I'm going
Is knowing where I'm coming from.

Chorus:
I don't want to be anything
Other than what I've been try'n' to be lately.
All I have to do is think of me,
And I have peace of mind.
I'm tired of looking 'round rooms wond'ring
What I've got to do,
Or who I'm supposed to be.
I don't want to be anything other than me.

Verse 2:
I'm surrounded by liars
Ev'rywhere I turn.
I'm surrounded by imposters
Ev'rywhere I turn.
I'm surrounded by identity crisis
Ev'rywhere I turn.
Am I the only one who noticed?
I can't be the only one who's learned.

Chorus:
I don't want to be anything
Other than what I've been try'n' to be lately.
All I have to do is think of me,
And I have peace of mind.
I'm tired of looking 'round rooms wond'ring
What I've got to do,
Or who I'm supposed to be.
I don't want to be anything other than me.

Bridge:
Can I have ev'ryone's attention, please?

*(Spoken:) If you're not like this and that,
You're gonna have to leave.*

I came from the mountain,
The crust of creation.
My whole situation made
From clay to stone, and
Now I'm tellin' ev'rybody.

Chorus:
I don't want to be anything
Other than what I've been try'n' to be lately.
All I have to do is think of me,
And I have peace of mind.
I'm tired of looking 'round rooms wond'ring
What I've got to do,
Or who I'm supposed to be.
I don't want to be anything other than me.

I don't want to be,
I don't want to be,
I don't want to be,
I don't want to be anything,
Anything other than me.

MACK THE KNIFE

(In the style of Bobby Darin)
English Words by MARC BLITZSTEIN, Original German Words by BERT BRECHT
Music by KURT WEILL

Verse 1:
Oh, the shark, babe, has such teeth, dear,
And he shows them pearly whites.
Just a jackknife has old Macheath, babe,
And he keeps it out of sight.

Verse 2:
You know when that shark bites with its teeth, babe,
Scarlet billows start to spread.
Fancy gloves, though, has old Macheath, babe,
So there's never, never a trace of red.

Verse 3:
Now, on the sidewalk, uh-huh, huh, ooh,
Sunday morning, uh-huh,
Lies a body just oozing life.
And someone's sneaking 'round the corner.
Could that someone be Mack the Knife?

Verse 4:
There's a tugboat down by the river, don't you know,
Where a cement bag's just a-droopin' on down.
Oh, that cement is just, it's there for the weight, dear.
Five'll get you ten, Old Mackie's back in town.

Verse 5:
Now, d'ja hear 'bout Louie Miller?
He disappeared, babe,
After drawing out all his hard-earned cash.
And now now, Macheath spends just like a sailor.
Could it be our boy's done something rash?

Verse 6:
Now, Jenny Diver, yeah, Sukey Tawdry,
Ooh, Miss Lotte Lenya, and old Lucy Brown.
Ooh, the line forms on the right, babe,
Now that Mackie's back in town.

Verse 7:
I said, Jenny Diver, Sukey Tawdry,
Look out to Miss Lotte Lenya, and old Lucy Brown.
Yes, that line forms on the right, babe,
Now that Mackie's back in town.

(Spoken:) Look out, old Mackie is back!

OPEN ARMS

(In the style of Journey)
Words and Music by STEVE PERRY and JONATHAN CAIN

Verse 1:
Lying beside you, here in the dark;
Feeling your heart beat with mine.
Softly you whisper; you're so sincere.
How could our love be so blind?
We sailed on together,
We drifted apart,
And here you are by my side.

Chorus:
So, now I come to you with open arms;
Nothing to hide, believe what I say.
So, here I am with open arms;
Hoping you see what your
Love means to me, open arms.

Verse 2:
Living without you, living alone,
This empty house seems so cold.
Wanting to hold you, wanting you near;
How much I wanted you home.
But now that you've come back,
Turned night into day,
I need you to stay.

Chorus:
So, now I come to you with open arms;
Nothing to hide, believe what I say.
So, here I am with open arms;
Hoping you'll see what your
Love means to me, open arms.

SMOOTH

(In the style of Rob Thomas)
Music and Lyrics by ITAAL SHUR and ROB THOMAS

Verse 1:
Man, it's a hot one,
Like seven inches from the mid-day sun.
Well, I hear you whisper and the words melt ev'ryone.
But you stay so cool.
My muñequita, my Spanish Harlem Mona Lisa.
You're my reason for reason, the step in my groove.

Pre-chorus:
And if you said this life ain't good enough,
I would give my world to lift you up.
I could change my life to better suit your mood.
'Cause you're so smooth.

Chorus:
Oh, and it's just like the ocean under the moon.
Well, it's the same as the emotion that I get from you.
You got the kind of loving that can be so smooth, yeah.
Give me your heart, make it real, or else forget about it.

Verse 2:
Well, I'll tell you one thing,
If you would leave, it be a crying shame.
In every breath and every word
I hear your name calling me out, yeah.
Well, out from the barrio,
You hear my rhythm on your radio.
You feel the tugging of the world,
So soft and slow, turning you 'round and 'round.

(Repeat Pre-chorus & Chorus)
(Guitar Solo)
(Repeat Chorus)

Or else forget about it. Or else forget about it.
Oh, let's don't forget about it.
Oh, let's don't forget about it.
(Repeat, ad lib)

WHEN A MAN LOVES A WOMAN

(In the style of Michael Bolton)
Words and Music by CALVIN LEWIS and ANDREW WRIGHT

Verse 1:
When a man loves a woman,
Can't keep his mind on nothin' else.
He'd trade the world
For the good thing he's found.
If she is bad, he can't see it.
She can do no wrong.
Turn his back on his best friend
If he puts her down.

Verse 2:
When a man loves a woman,
Spend his very last dime
Trying to hold on to what he needs.
He'd give up all his comforts,
Sleep out in the rain,
If she said that's the way
It ought to be.

Bridge:
Yeah, when a man loves a woman, yeah,
I give you everything I've got, oh, oh.
Trying to hold on
To your precious love.
Baby, baby, please don't treat me bad.

Verse 3:
When a man loves a woman,
Deep down in his soul,
She can bring him such misery.
If she is playing him for a fool,
He's the last one to know.
Loving eyes can never see.

Verse 4:
Yes, when a man loves a woman,
I know exactly how he feels,
'Cause, baby, baby, ooh.

When a man loves a woman, oh.
When a man loves a woman, yeah.
When a man loves a woman.
When a man, when a man,
When a man loves a woman.

WHAT A WONDERFUL WORLD

(In the style of Louis Armstrong)
Words and Music by GEORGE DAVID WEISS and BOB THIELE

I see trees of green, red roses too,
I see them bloom for me and you,
And I think to myself
What a wonderful world.

I see skies of blue and clouds of white,
The bright blessed day, the dark sacred night,
And I think to myself
What a wonderful world.

The colors of the rainbow, so pretty in the sky
Are also on the faces of people goin' by,
I see friends shakin' hands, sayin', "How do you do!"
They're really sayin', "I love you."

I hear babies cry, I watch them grow,
They'll learn much more than I'll ever know
And I think to myself what a wonderful world.
Yes I think to myself
What a wonderful world.

WHEN THE STARS GO BLUE

(In the style of Tim McGraw)
Words and Music by RYAN ADAMS

Verse 1:
Dancin' when the stars go blue.
Dancin' when the evening fell.
Dancin' in your wooden shoes in a wedding gown.

Verse 2:
Dancin' out on seventh street.
Dancin' through the underground.
Dancin' with the marionette, are you happy now?

Chorus:
Where do you go when you're lonely?
Where do you go when you're blue?
Where do you go when you're lonely?
I'll follow you when the stars go blue,
Stars go blue, stars go blue, stars go blue.

Verse 3:
Laughing with your pretty mouth.
Laughing with your broken eyes.
Laughing with your lover's tongue in a lullaby.

Chorus:
Where do you go when you're lonely?
Where do you go when you're blue?
Where do you go when you're lonely?
I'll follow you when the stars go blue,
Stars go blue, stars go blue, stars go blue.

YOU RAISE ME UP

(In the style of Josh Groban)
Words and Music by ROLF LOVLAND and BRENDAN GRAHAM

Verse:
When I am down, and oh, my soul so weary,
When troubles come and my heart burdened be,
Then I am still and wait here in the silence
Until you come and sit a while with me.

Chorus:
You raise me up
So I can stand on mountains.
You raise me up
To walk on stormy seas.
I am strong
When I am on your shoulders.
You raise me up
To more than I can be.

(Instrumental 8 bars)

Chorus:
You raise me up
So I can stand on mountains.
You raise me up
To walk on stormy seas.
I am strong
When I am on your shoulders.
You raise me up
To more than I can be.

You raise me up
So I can stand on mountains.
You raise me up
To walk on stormy seas.
I am strong
When I am on your shoulders.
You raise me up
To more than I can be.

You raise me up
So I can stand on mountains.
You raise me up
To walk on stormy seas.
I am strong
When I am on your shoulders.
You raise me up
To more than I can be.

You raise me up
To more than I can be.